MAPS

Kay Robertson

Rourke
Educational Media

rourkeeducationalmedia.com

www.rourkeeducationalmedia.com

PHOTO CREDITS: Cover: Urszula Sawicka; page 1: © binabina; page 4: © Ampack; page 8: © GooDween123; page 10: © Mledbetter24; page 11: © AdrianHillman; page 13: © GlobalStock; page 14: © Sandamali Fernando; page 15: © GoAnywherePhoto; page 16: © Nikada; page 17: © Giuseppemarchi; page 18: © Giuseppemarchi; page 20: © Pincarel Graphics; page 21: © Mike_kiev; page 22: © David Francisco; page 24, 43: ©Ablestock.com @Getty Images; page 26: © dagsjo; page 28: © bruceman; page 29: © Spvvkr; page 30: © caracterdesign; page 31: © richcarey; page 32: © MCCAIG; page 33: © Michael Schmeling; page 34: Courtesy NOAA; page 35: © IZO; page 36: © rwarnick; page 38: © Orlando Florin Rosu; page 39: © jamesbenet; page 40: © John A Davis; page 41: © NASA; page 42: © Trout55; page 44: © acitore

Editor: Jill Sherman

Cover and interior design by Tara Raymo

Library of Congress PCN Data

STEM Guides to Maps / Kay Robertson.
    p. cm. -- (STEM Everyday)
Includes index.
ISBN 978-1-62169-845-6 (hardcover)
ISBN 978-1-62169-740-4 (softcover)
ISBN 978-1-62169-948-4 (e-Book)
Library of Congress Control Number: 2013936450

Also Available as:
ROURKE'S
e-Books

Rourke Educational Media
Printed in the United States of America,
North Mankato, Minnesota

Rourke
Educational Media

rourkeeducationalmedia.com

customerservice@rourkeeducationalmedia.com • PO Box 643328 Vero Beach, Florida 32964

Table of Contents

Introduction

People use maps all the time and for good reason. Maps make it easy to find out where you are and how to get to where you want to go. This is called navigation, the process of directing cars, boats, airplanes, and even people.

When was the last time you used a map to get somewhere? Can you think of ways that math relates to maps?

If you ever find yourself in a big, unfamiliar place like a park, train station, or shopping mall, the simplest way to orient yourself is to find a map. Often times, a map will be posted with your locaton clearly labeled as "you are here."

Maybe you never knew it, but maps depend on math for their accuracy. Most maps are created to help people travel great distances. Because of this, the details on a map have to be precise. Math guarantees this precision.

This map shows a portion of downtown New York City.

Considering Scale

Maps are like pictures that show you places and things from angles that you don't typically see in real life. The most common angle for a map is a view from far above, which is sometimes called a bird's eye view.

But, a map is much more than just a picture because it is meant to show very specific information. Photos of New York taken from above don't look much like maps. The streets aren't labeled. Roads are not highlighted and places of interest are not identified.

A topographic photo showing the southwest corner of New York City's Central Park.

So although a map is a picture, it is a picture meant to convey specific information like **distance**, direction, or elevation. Calculating distance is one of the most common uses for a map. Maps make this an easy task because they are drawn to scale.

But what does drawn to scale mean?

Essentially, it means that the place the map shows is a different size than the map. This is done for practical reasons. A map of the United States that was the exact same size of the United States wouldn't be very useful. To start with, you wouldn't be able to store it anywhere!

Instead, people rely on maps that depict large areas on a smaller scale. Maps use a small measurement to depict a larger measurement.

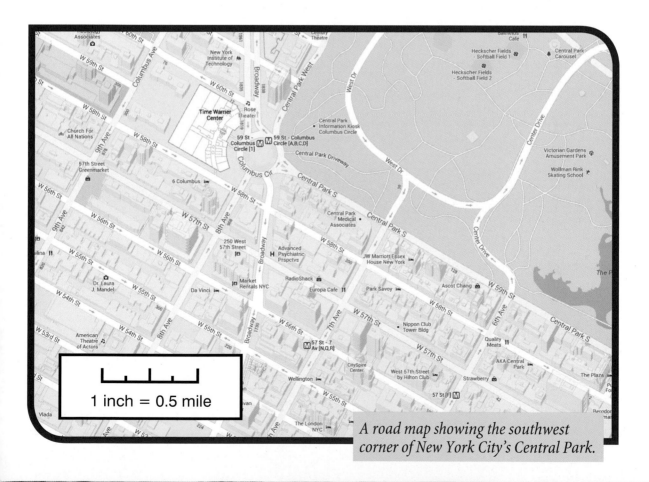

1 inch = 0.5 mile

A road map showing the southwest corner of New York City's Central Park.

STEM in Action?

Have you ever wondered how big the United States is? You can find out by using a map.

Your map of the United States might use a different scale, but for the purposes of this example, imagine that the scale of the map is 1 inch equals 150 miles.

Using a ruler, find out how many inches there are between the West Coast of the United States and the East Coast.

Your map might be different, but in this case, let's say there are about 18 inches from the West Coast to the East Coast. To convert this distance from inches to miles, all you have to do is multiply the number of inches by the scale:

$$18 \times 150 = 2{,}700$$

So the United States is about 2,700 miles across!

Now that you know the distance across the United States, what about the distance from top to bottom?

This is a little trickier than measuring the distance across, because this time there isn't a specific stopping point like the Atlantic and Pacific oceans.

Your answer should be **1,575**.

Now that you have those two calculations, you can calculate the **area** of the United States. That is to say, the measure of the total land mass.

To calculate this figure, you need to multiply the distance across by the distance from top to bottom. The results will be in square miles:

2,700 x 1,575 = 4,252,500

So the total area of the United States is about 4,252,500 square miles! To make things simpler, you can also round that number down and say that the total area of the United States is about 4 million square miles.

As you can see, maps are very useful for measuring distances, which is why they come in handy when planning a trip. **Direction** is another reason why maps are so useful. It's good to know how far away your destination is when you begin a trip. But unless you know what direction to travel in, you might as well stay home.

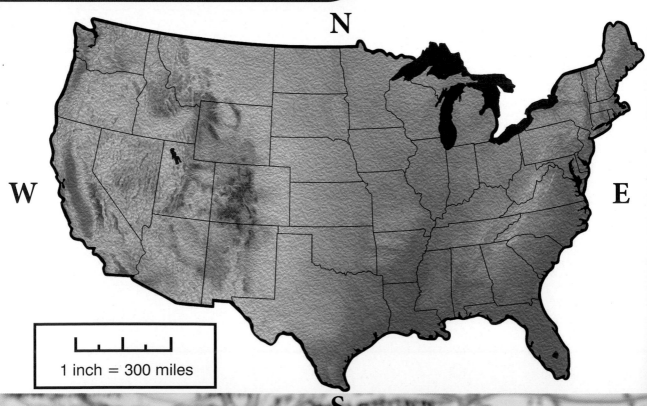

1 inch = 300 miles

STEM Fast Fact !

Legends

Very detailed maps often come with **legends**. A legend is a box on the map, usually placed in one of the corners, that explains what the symbols or icons on the map mean.

Some standard map icons include:

H The letter H represents a hospital

✈ An airplane represents an airport

⛺ A tent repsresent a campground

Can you think of other symbols that might appear on a map legend and what they would stand for?

H	Hospital
✈	Airport
⛺	Campground
+–+–+	Railroad
▬▬	Road
══	Highway
▬▬	Waterway

Using a Compass

Did you know that the Earth is a giant magnet? Like a magnet, the Earth has a North Pole and South Pole. The North Pole is called the Arctic. The South Pole, on the other hand, is called Antarctica.

It is because of Earth's magnetic properties that people can use compasses. With the right map and a compass, you can find your way just about anywhere in the world.

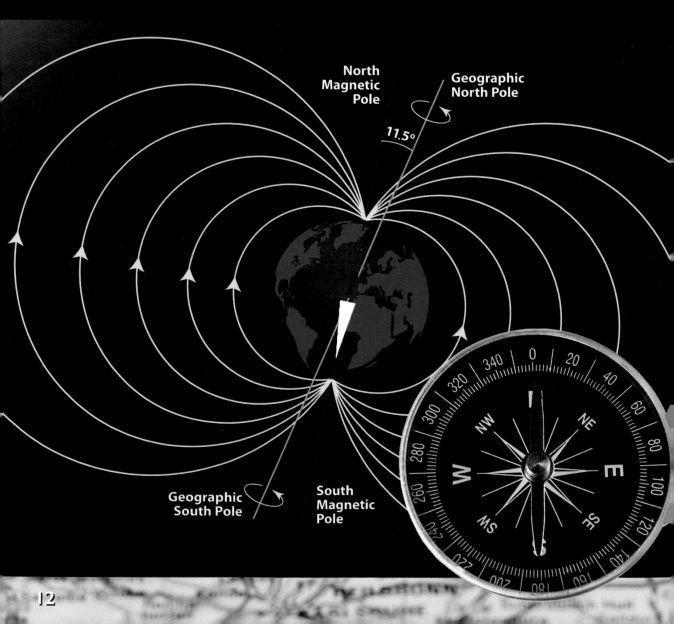

A compass is an instrument that you are probably already familiar with, even if you do not know how it works. A compass is a magnet. More specifically, the directional needle on a compass is a magnet. One end of the needle is usually painted. The needle turns in reaction to the Earth's magnetism and the painted end always points north.

STEM in Action **?**

A typical compass indicates the four basic directions:

N – North
S – South
E – East
W – West

These directions always point in the same way:

North – Top
South – Bottom
East – Right
West – Left

With north defined by the compass needle, you can also determine which direction is south, east, or west.

If you look more closely at the compass, you will see that it is also labeled with numbers. These are **degrees** of direction. Degrees are a unit of measurement developed by the ancient Greeks. They divide a circle into 360 portions, or degrees. Degrees are like very thin slices of a circle.

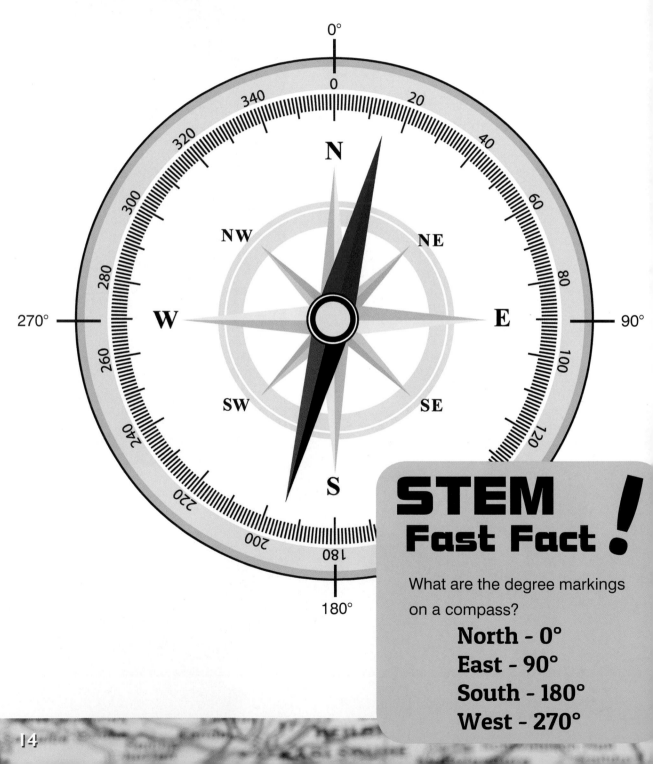

STEM Fast Fact!

What are the degree markings on a compass?

North - 0°
East - 90°
South - 180°
West - 270°

The difference in degrees between each of the four directions is exactly 90 degrees. These numbers are all multiples. More specifically, they are multiples of 90.

90°	90°
90°	90°

In order to make one full turn, or revolution, you have to travel from 0, to 90 degrees, to 180 degrees, to 270 degrees, and finally to 360 degrees, which is really returning to zero. Have you ever spun yourself around in a circle? You actually spun your body 360 degrees, which is one complete revolution!

Things that travel in a circular motion, like this Ferris wheel, travel in degrees. If one full revolution of the Ferris wheel is equal to 360 degrees, how many degrees are there in a half revolution? A quarter?

Some compasses also include four other directions, which are really just combinations of the first four:

NE – Northeast
NW – Northwest
SE – Southeast
SW – Southwest

You already know that the number of degrees between north and east is 90. How many degrees, then, is northeast?

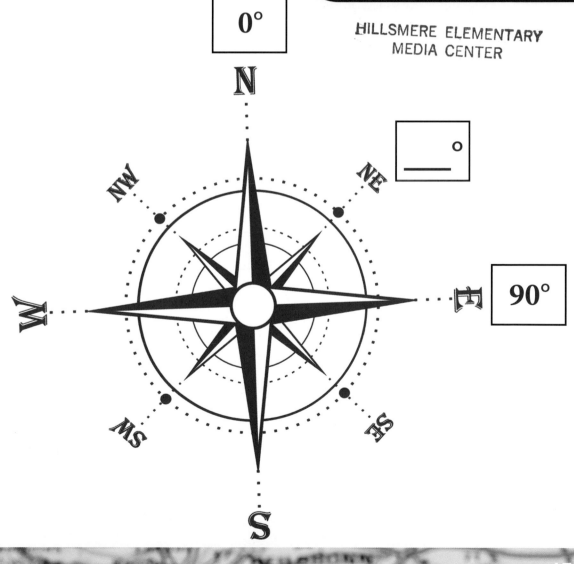

0°

HILLSMERE ELEMENTARY
MEDIA CENTER

_____ °

90°

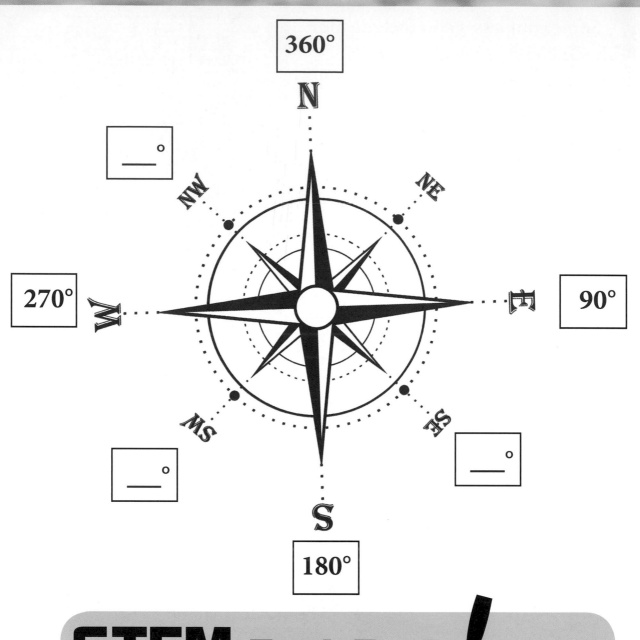

STEM Fast Fact!

The Compass Rose

Sometimes maps will include a compass rose to indicate which way is north.

A compass rose is a two-dimensional representation of a compass. However, a compass rose isn't functional. Turning the map will not cause the compass rose to change position.

In older maps particularly, the compass rose is often highly stylized and decorated.

STEM in Action ?

Can you determine the degrees for other three combined directions: southeast, northwest, and sorthwest? Southeast is midway between east and south.

To find the degree measure of southeast, add up east and south and divide by two:

$$90 + 180 = 270$$
$$270 \div 2 = 135$$

Southeast is at approximately 135 degrees. How about southwest?

$$180 + 270 = 450$$
$$450 \div 2 = 225$$

Southwest is at 225 degrees.

And, finally, can you calculate the degrees for northwest? Northwest is a little tricky, since you may think that it is somewhere between 270 degrees and zero degrees. Remember, though, that one complete revolution is 360 degrees. Those are the two numbers you must use to calculate northwest:

$$270 + 360 = 630$$
$$630 \div 2 = 315$$

So northwest is at 315 degrees!

Here's our complete chart:

North – 0°
Northeast – 45°
East – 90°
Southeast – 135°
South – 180°
Southwest – 225°
West – 270°
Northwest – 315°

Longitude and Latitude

Considering that the Earth is round, doesn't it seem a little odd that many of the maps we use to represent the Earth are flat? The fact is, it's impossible to represent a round object like the Earth on a flat map without creating distortion. Distortion causes some of the Earth's continents to appear larger or smaller on a flat map than they really are.

Globes are some of the most accurate maps that exist. This is because the Earth is a three-dimensional object that is close to spherical. A globe is an accurate representation of the spherical shape of the world.

The solution developed for this problem was to represent the Earth on another round object, a globe!

The Earth and the globes used to represent it are spheres.

In the last section, you learned about degrees and how they apply to the measurement of a circle. Degrees also apply to the measurement of spheres.

Have you ever cut an orange right down the middle?

You end up with two orange halves. That's a little bit like how the Earth is divided. Actually, it is divided twice.

The first division takes place from north to south. Imagine a line starting from the North Pole, traveling through Great Britain, Europe, Africa, and down to Antarctica. This line is known as the prime meridian, and it represents 0 degrees. Meanwhile, on the other side of the Earth, the same line continues, but there it is not called the prime meridian. Instead, it is called the 180-degree line.

Prime Meridian

This might seem confusing, but look at your compass again. Imagine that the compass is the Earth viewed from above. If the center of the compass is the North Pole, then 0 degrees would be the line of the prime meridian, and the same line returning to the North Pole on the other side would be at 180 degrees.

All of the measurements in between the prime meridian and the 180-degree line are known as degrees of **longitude**. Degrees of longitude are represented by vertical lines.

But the Earth is actually divided twice. The second dividing line measures around the Earth like a belt. This line is called the equator. The equator divides the Earth in half and functions as 0 degrees. Meanwhile, the North Pole, the top of the world, would be at 90 degrees north and the South Pole, the bottom of the world, would be at 90 degrees south.

Every degree in between the equator and either of Earth's poles represents a measurement of **latitude**. Areas north of the equator are measured at degrees north latitude. Areas south of the equator are measured at degrees south latitude.

STEM in Action ?

In between degrees of longitude or latitude are even smaller measurements called minutes. In every degree there are sixty minutes. If there are 90 degrees between the equator to the North Pole, how many minutes is that?

You can find out by multiplying:

90 x 60 = 5,400

There are 5,400 minutes between the equator and the North Pole!

Any place on Earth can be located by specifying degrees and minutes of latitude and longitude. The symbol for degrees is °, while the symbol for minutes is ´. Here, for instance, is the location of Bangor, a city in Maine:

City	State	Latitude		Longitude	
Bangor	Maine	44°	48´	68°	47´

You can read this data as, 44 degrees 48 minutes north latitude, 68 degrees 47 minutes west longitude. The readings any place in United States will be in degrees north latitude and west longitude. This is because the continent of North America is above, or north, of the equator and west of the prime meridian.

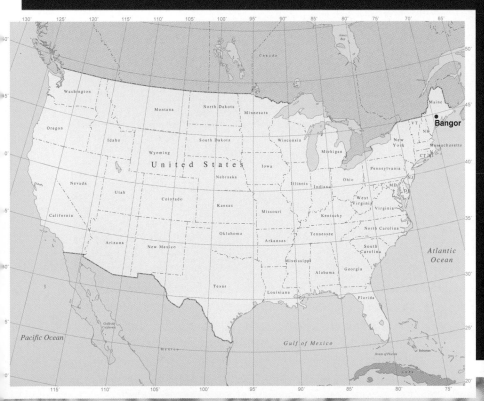

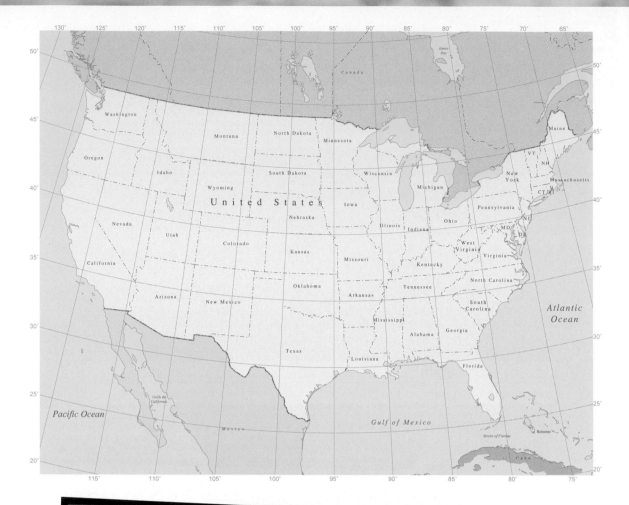

Any location can be determined using degrees of longitude and latitude. For example, the city of Boston, pictured here, is located at 42° 22' north latitude and 71° 2' west longitude. How does that compare with the city of Bismarck, North Dakota, located at 46° 46' north latitude and 100° 45' west longitude?

STEM in Action ?

Take a look at some more cities of the United States located by latitude and longitude. Here is a list of five cities:

City	State	Latitude		Longitude	
Montgomery	Alabama	32°	22′	86°	18′
Juneau	Alaska	58°	18′	134°	25′
Phoenix	Arizona	33°	26′	112°	4′
Little Rock	Arkansas	34°	44′	92°	17′
Sacramento	California	38°	34′	121°	29′

You can compare the measurements of longitude for each city:

Juneau, Alaska: 134° 25′
Montgomery, Alabama: 86° 18′

Just to make things simpler, drop the minutes:

Juneau, Alaska: 134°
Montgomery, Alabama: 86°

Now subtract the smaller number from the larger number:

134 – 86 = 48°

Juneau, Alaska is about 48 degrees west of Montgomery, Alabama!

About how far north is Juneau, Alaska, compared to Montgomery, Alabama? To find out, compare the latitudes of each city, dropping the minutes:

Juneau, Alaska: 58°
Montgomery, Alabama: 32°

Then subtract the smaller number from the larger number:

58 – 32 = 26°

Juneau, Alaska, is 26 degrees north of Montgomery, Alabama!

Put the readings for latitude and longitude together, and you can say that Juneau, Alaska, is 48 degrees west, 26 degrees north of Montgomery, Alabama!

Measuring Elevation

Have you ever climbed a mountain? Maybe you and your family have done this on a summer vacation.

If you look at the right map, you can probably find the mountain you climbed. It may appear as a little triangle along with the mountain's height. Just as maps can be used to express distance and direction, they can also be used to express **elevation**.

Mount McKinley

Maps can also be used to specify elevation. If, for example, a map told you that the tallest mountain of this range reaches 15,000 feet, what is it 15,000 feet above?

The word elevation may remind you of the word elevator. That's a good association, because an elevator takes you up.

In the case of an elevator, the floors are all being compared to the ground floor, or first floor. For example, the third floor of a building is two stories higher than the first floor.

Mountains are also measured in terms of elevation. But what are their heights being compared to? Unlike an elevator, there isn't a first floor on a mountain!

The missing link here is sea level.

Sea level is the level of the sea. Sea level isn't a fixed number. The approximate sea level is the starting point for measuring elevation. Sea level, then, is zero, and anything higher than sea level is above sea level.

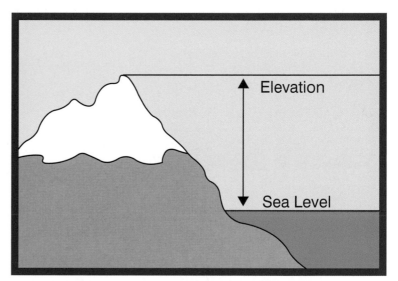

Rank #	Name	State	Height (feet)
1	Mount McKinley	Alaska	20,320
2	Mount St. Elias	Alaska	18,008
3	Mount Foraker	Alaska	17,400
4	Mount Bona	Alaska	16,500
5	Mount Blackburn	Alaska	16,390
6	Mount Sanford	Alaska	16,237
7	Mount Vancouver	Alaska	15,979
8	South Buttress	Alaska	15,885
9	Mount Churchill	Alaska	15,638
10	Mount Fairweather	Alaska	15,300

How many more feet above sea level is Mount McKinley compared to Mount St. Elias?

You can find out by subtracting the smaller number from the larger number:

$$20,320 - 18,008 = 2,312$$

Mount McKinley rises up about 2,312 feet higher than Mount St. Elias!

Mount Whitney reaches up 14,494 feet above sea level. Compare that with the height of Mount McKinley.

$$20,320 - 14,494 = 5,826$$

So, Mount Whitney is about 5,826 feet lower than Mount McKinley.

Elevation is usually measured in feet above sea level. Mount McKinley, for instance, is 20,320 feet (6,193 meters) high. That means that Mount McKinley is 20,320 feet (6,193 meters) above sea level.

Mount St. Elias, on the other hand, rises up to 18,008 feet (5,488 meters) above sea level.

Mount Elias

Maybe you've noticed that all of these mountains are in Alaska. What is the highest mountain peak in the United States outside of Alaska? The highest mountain in the United States outside of Alaska is Mount Whitney in California.

Mount Whitney

There is no such thing as a perfectly accurate number for sea level. However, with the aid of special instruments like satellites and stilling wells, an approximate reading is possible.

STEM Fast Fact!

Measuring Sea Level

Sea level is something that is constantly changing. This is due to factors like temperature, rainfall, and the tides.

As you can imagine, all of these factors make determining the sea level extremely difficult. So how do scientists do it?

One method of finding the sea level is by using a device called a stilling well. It is a thick length of pipe with a hole in the middle. While the waters outside the pipe may shift, the water that drains into the pipe remains stable, making a fairly accurate reading of the sea level possible. Scientists have also begun using satellites to calculate the sea level.

Neither of these methods is foolproof, but the readings they give us can be trusted within a small margin of error.

Measuring Depth

In the previous section, you learned about maps that describe elevation. Now you're going to learn about **depths**, or measurements that go below sea level.

A ray is a fish species that lives at the bottom of the sea.

STEM Fast Fact!

Ocean	Average Depth (Feet)	Greatest Known Depth (Feet)	Place of Greatest Known Depth
Pacific Ocean	13,215	36,198	Mariana Trench
Atlantic Ocean	12,880	30,246	Puerto Rico
Indian Ocean	13,002	24,460	Sunda Trench
Arctic Ocean	3,953	18,456	77°45´N; 175°W

Source - www.infoplease.com

The Pacific Ocean is an **average** of 13,215 feet (4,027 meters) deep. But what does that mean?

If you went to the edge of a beach on the Pacific Ocean, where the land meets the sea, the water there wouldn't be 13,000 feet (3,962.4 meters) deep. That is because 13,000 feet (3,962.4 meters) deep is just an average depth of the Pacific Ocean. An average is a number that represents a group of numbers.

But in order to calculate the average depth, scientists have to know the depths of all parts of the ocean. The ocean's greatest known depth is not an average. You can compare the greatest depth of a particular ocean with the average depth of that ocean.

STEM in Action ?

Using the chart, can you figure out how much deeper the Pacific Ocean is compared to the Atlantic Ocean? You can find out by subtracting the smaller number from the larger number:

13,215 – 12,880 = 335

So the average depth of the Pacific Ocean is roughly 335 feet deeper than the Atlantic Ocean!

The deepest portion of the Indian Ocean is the Sunda Trench, which reaches 24,460 feet below sea level. How much deeper is this compared to the average depth of the Indian Ocean, measured at 13,002 feet?

To find out, just subtract the smaller number from the larger number:

24,460 – 13,002 = 11,458

The Sunda Trench reaches 11,458 feet deeper than the average depth of the Indian Ocean!

Samatra

Sunda Trench

Java

The greatest known depth of any ocean, is the Mariana Trench, located in the Pacific Ocean. This trench reaches 36,198 feet (11,033 meters) below sea level.

CHINA

TAIWAN

Pacific Ocean

PHILIPPINES

← **Mariana Trench**

STEM in Action ?

Fathoms

Sometimes, the sea is measured in fathoms. A **fathom** is a unit of measurement equal to six feet.

How deep is the Mariana Trench in terms of fathoms? You can find out by dividing the measurement for the trench in feet by the number of feet in one fathom:

$$36{,}198 \div 6 = 6{,}033$$

The Mariana Trench is 6,033 fathoms deep!

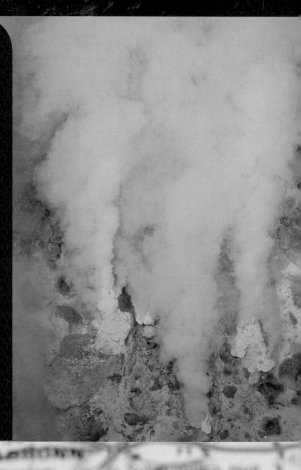

STEM in Action ?

In one mile there are 5,280 feet. How many miles below sea level, then, does the Mariana Trench reach?

You can find out by dividing the depth of the Mariana Trench by the number of feet in one mile:

$$36{,}198 \div 5{,}280 = 6.85$$

The Mariana Trench reaches almost seven miles below sea level!

Mariana Trench

Our Solar System

Did you know that maps can also be used to represent outer space? If you have ever looked at a map of our solar system you already know this.

Don't forget that maps are primarily used for navigation. Just as mankind has explored planet Earth, the human race is only just beginning to explore outer space. Space is a pretty big place, but maps help to make it understandable.

Ea

Mercury

Venus

The word solar refers to the Sun. A solar system is made up of a star, like the Sun, and the planets that orbit, or circle, around it.

Once you leave Earth, there is no point in measuring distances in terms of miles. Things in outer space are so far apart that miles are simply too small a unit of measurement. Instead, scientists measure space distances in terms of astronomical units (AU).

The astronomical unit is based on the distance from the Sun to the Earth. This distance is equal to 92.9 million miles.

Jupiter

Uranus

Neptune

Saturn

Mars

Try This

Can you name the eight planets of our solar system? Here they are, in order of increasing distance from the Sun:

    Mercury

    Venus

    Earth

    Mars

    Jupiter

    Saturn

    Uranus

    Neptune

STEM
Fast Fact!

Pluto used to be considered a planet. It was the smallest planet in our solar system. Scientists now call it a dwarf planet, leaving our solar system with just eight planets.

STEM in Action ?

How far away from Earth is Neptune? You can find out by comparing each planet's astronomical unit measure. Just subtract the smaller number from the larger number:

$$30.1 - 1 = 29.1$$

Neptune is 29.1 astronomical units from the Earth.

What if you wanted to know each planet's distance from the Sun in miles?

All you would have to do is multiply the planet's astronomical unit measure by the number of miles in one astronomical unit (92.9 million):

Mercury – .04 AU x 92,900,000

Venus – .07 AU x 92,900,000

Earth – 1 AU x 92,900,000

Mars – 1.5 AU x 92,900,000

Jupiter – 5.2 AU x 92,900,000

Saturn – 9.6 AU x 92,900,000

Uranus – 19.2 AU x 92,900,000

Neptune – 30.1 AU x 92,900,000

Sun

Mercury

Venus

Earth

Planet	Distance from the Sun
Mercury	.04 AU
Venus	.07 AU
Earth	1 AU
Mars	1.5 AU
Jupiter	5.2 AU
Saturn	9.6 AU
Uranus	19.2 AU
Neptune	30.1 AU

Mars   Jupiter   Saturn   Uranus   Neptune

Notice anything strange about this globe? It is actually a map of the moon, not the Earth! As you can see, the moon does not have any oceans, although it does have a number of deep craters.

STEM in Action?

Now calculate the results. Are you sure you're ready? These are going to be some big numbers!

Mercury – 3,716,000 miles from the Sun
Venus – 6,503,000 miles from the Sun
Earth – 92,900,000 miles from the Sun
Mars – 139,350,000 miles from the Sun
Jupiter – 483,080,000 miles from the Sun
Saturn – 891,840,000 miles from the Sun
Uranus – 1,783,680,000 miles from the Sun
Neptune – 2,796,290,000 miles from the Sun

Now you know why it's easier for scientists to measure distances in space with astronomical units!

STEM Fast Fact!

The Hubble Telescope

Since the earliest days of astronomy, astronomers have shared a single goal, to see more, see farther, see deeper.

The Hubble Space Telescope's launch in 1990 was one of humanity's greatest advances in that goal. Hubble is one of NASA's most successful and long-lasting science missions. It has beamed hundreds of thousands of images back to Earth, shedding light on many of the great mysteries of astronomy. Its gaze has helped determine the age of the universe, the identity of quasars, and the existence of dark energy.

Conclusion

Who is responsible for creating all the maps that people depend on to guide them?

People who research, design, and create maps are called cartographers. The science of creating maps is known as **cartography**.

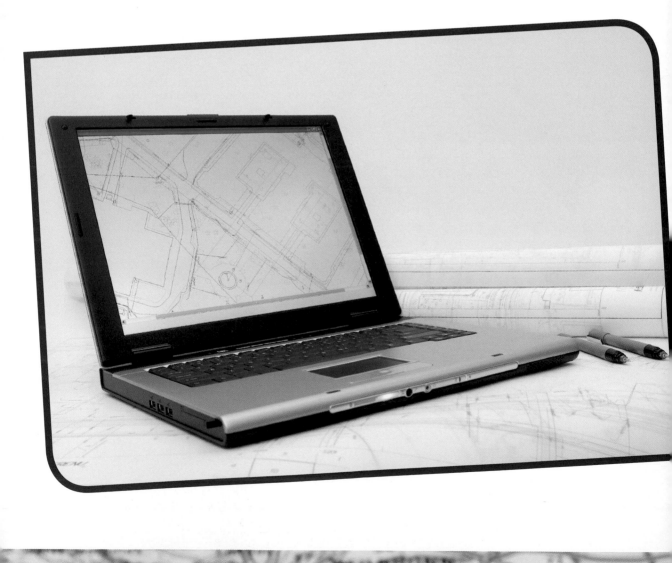

Pictured here is an old world map with some of the navigational tools used in ancient times.

If you have found this book interesting, maybe you will want to consider a career in cartography! You can be part of the future of mapmaking. Maybe you'll create maps of portions of the ocean or maps detailing the surface of other planets!

All you need is math!

Glossary

area (AIR-ee-uh): a measure of the total land mass in a space

average (AV-ur-ij): a number used to represent a group of numbers

cartography (kahr-TAH-gruh-fee): the science of designing and creating maps

degrees (di-GREEZ): very small divisions of a circle

depths (depths): measurements below sea level

direction (duh-REK-shuhn): the line along which something moves

distance (DIS-tuhns): the space between two places

elevation (el-uh-VAY-shuhn): height; measurements above sea level

fathoms (FATH-uhms): a measure of depth equal to six feet

latitude (LAT-i-tood): horizontal degrees of measurement

legend (LEJ-uhnd): a reference explaining what the symbols on a map represent

longitude (LAHN-ji-tood): vertical degrees of measurement

Index

Metric System

We actually have two systems of weights and measures in the United States. Quarts, pints, gallons, ounces, and pounds are all units of the U.S. Customary System, also known as the Imperial System.

The other system of measurement, and the only one sanctioned by the United States Government, is the metric system, which is also known as the International System of Units. French scientists developed the metric system in the 1790s. The basic unit of measurement in the metric system is the meter, which is about one ten-millionth the distance from the North Pole to the equator.

A metal bar used to represent the length of the standard meter was even created. This bar was replaced in the 1980s, though, when scientists changed the standard of measurement for the meter to a portion of the distance traveled by light in a vacuum.

Converting Imperial to Metric			
Convert	To	Multiply by	Example
inches (in)	millimeters (mm)	25.40	2in x 25.40 = 50.8mm
inches (in)	centimeters (cm)	2.54	2in x 2.54 = 5.08cm
feet (ft)	meters (m)	0.30	2ft x .30 = 0.6m
yards (yd)	meters (m)	0.91	2yd x .91 = 1.82m
miles (mi)	kilometers (km)	1.61	2mi x 1.61 = 3.22km
miles per hour (mph)	kilometers per hour (km/h)	1.61	2mph x 1.61 = 3.22km/h
ounces (oz)	grams (g)	28.35	2oz x 28.35 = 56.7g
pounds (lb)	kilograms (kg)	0.454	2lb x .454 = 0.908kg
tons (T)	metric ton (MT)	1.016	2T x 1.016 = 2.032
ounces (oz)	milliliters (ml)	29.57	2oz x 29.57 = 59.14ml
pint (pt)	liter (l)	0.55	2pt x .55 = 1.1l
quarts (qt)	liters (l)	0.95	2qt x .95 = 1.9l
gallons (gal)	liters (l)	3.785	2gal x 3.785 = 7.57

Websites to Visit

www.nypl.org/research/chss/epo/mapexhib/map.html
New York Public Library – How To Read a Map

www.howstuffworks.com/compass.htm
How Stuff Works – How Compasses Work

www.infoplease.com/ipa/A0001796.html
Infoplease – Latitude and Longitude of U.S. and Canadian Cities

Show What You Know

1. Define sea level.

2. Define elevation.

3. What is the deepest known trench in the world?

4. Why do scientists use AUs to measure distances in space?

5. How does a compass work?